Psalms for Skeptics

Psalms for Skeptics

(101–150)

KENT GRAMM

RESOURCE *Publications* · Eugene, Oregon

PSALMS FOR SKEPTICS
(101–150)

Copyright © 2014 Kent Gramm. All rights reserved. Except for brief quotations in critical publications or reviews, no part of this book may be reproduced in any manner without prior written permission from the publisher. Write: Permissions. Wipf and Stock Publishers, 199 W. 8th Ave., Suite 3, Eugene, OR 97401.

Resource Publications
An Imprint of Wipf and Stock Publishers
199 W. 8th Ave., Suite 3
Eugene, OR 97401

www.wipfandstock.com

ISBN 13: 978-1-62564-853-2

Manufactured in the U.S.A.   09/11/2014

for Ruth

Contents

Psalm 101 | 1
Psalm 102 | 2
Psalm 103 | 6
Psalm 104 | 7
Psalm 105 | 8
Psalm 106 | 11
Psalm 107 | 14
Psalm 108 | 19
Psalm 109 | 20
Psalm 110 | 21
Psalm 111 | 23
Psalm 112 | 26
Psalm 114 | 32
Psalm 115 | 36
Psalm 116 | 38
Psalm 117 | 39
Psalm 118 | 40
Psalm 119 | 43
Psalm 120 | 58
Psalm 121 | 60
Psalm 122 | 66
Psalm 123 | 68
Psalm 124 | 71
Psalm 125 | 75
Psalm 126 | 79

Psalm 127 | 80
Psalm 128 | 82
Psalm 129 | 86
Psalm 130 | 89
Psalm 131 | 98
Psalm 132 | 99
Psalm 133 | 104
Psalm 134 | 105
Psalm 135 | 107
Psalm 136 | 108
Psalm 137 | 115
Psalm 138 | 120
Psalm 139 | 124
Psalm 140 | 137
Psalm 141 | 140
Psalm 142 | 141
Psalm 143 | 142
Psalm 143 | 146
Psalm 144 | 153
Psalm 145 | 154
Psalm 146 | 157
Psalm 147 | 160
Psalm 148 | 162
Psalm 149 | 165
Psalm 150 | 168

Psalm 101

O when wilt thou come unto me?   (Advent)

You come, I go: one sight of the white Light
and this body drops alone, familiar bone
cold forever, an undertaker's stone
in a lake of my children's tears. All right.
What's left to want but a sign, some surprise,
kindness where the waters of memory
part, Jesus? When you do come unto me—
materialize to my lidded eyes—
what will I be? How will I see what I
don't want to see? What I am afraid of
is what I want: the unsupposed glory
that penetrates light, the postponed beauty,
the starry child of everlasting love,
the face of truth, beneficent and gory.

Psalm 102

My heart is smitten

My heart is smitten. Something happened here,
inside, like a fire blown out with a bang.
Fell, turned green, passed out. It wasn't a scare:
it was the real thing. The fat lady sang
like a locomotive. Me, on a cart,
an hour from dead. They put me on a table
and Jesus ran a wire into my heart,
opened a tube; stepped back into fable—
but I knew. He was there. He left a sign,
an artifact, a feather: I mean me.
I was immortal once upon a time,
bore frankincense; unique, I used to be.
But now I see I am a different self.
Survived for now, like everybody else.

Psalm 102

> *my days are consumed like smoke*

I can't hear it, but I know it is ticking.
The days go by with nothing done. Like smoke
from a wispy fire—some dust-thin poems
going out before they reach the flickering
burn. Complain, why don't I?—that would burn
still more of what is left, a paper tear
on a paper face in a paper year
in a paper space. Do they also serve
who only sit and waste? But let Indian
Summer come, the lazy childhood haze,
bracing fragrant taste of leaves in the smoke,
maples grateful to the all-gracious sun,
and remembering youth going where it goes
uncompleted, ripe, and smiling away.

Psalms for Skeptics

I am in trouble

My heart is stricken: I will lose you all.
"Where I am going, none of you may go."
What's worse is where that is, none of us knows;
still worse, we all know. Whatever you call
it, it smells of flowers for awhile, dust
on the face, the mortician's after shave:
what theological word rhymes with "grave"
that doesn't tremble on the lip of "lost"?

One night the Lord came to me in my sleep,
looking handsome like David the Great King,
O Israel, whose look, more powerful
than horses, calls the universe like sheep
from particles, Eternity in flower;
and I was saved. And I will be waiting.

Psalm 102

But thou, O Lord, shalt endure forever.

The only comfort is the only comfort.
For what is hell but life eternal—that's
it; just life eternal. Live forever,
enemy! Just you and your friends. Quiet.
Except for an exploding star now and
then, cosmos expanding like an apple
a thousand miles per second, the random
black hole gulping like a hollow drain, and
so on and so on. You will get damn sick
of your friends. Go see the fireworks every
night, all night; one long night. You will all wish
you were dead. That this satire of heaven
 would have had a Maker. That the humming
 in all that dark matter would mean something.

Psalm 103

Bless the Lord, O my soul

O bless the Lord, my soul, whoever you
may be, you keeper of our memories:
you, whom I call mine though I am yours—I,
the day-to-day perception and illusion,
the child of the unconscious mind, body's
bedfellow, servant, and traducer, dead
in a sweet dream of aphrodesia, dead
in the lost cause of astronomy: me,
loved?—not the clothes horse I know. But someone
I don't know who knows me is loved: you
the aromatic of the lotus rose,
beloved of the one and only One,
loved, loved—and you know what I only wound
and crucify: bless the Lord, O my soul!

Psalm 104

thou art clothed with honor and majesty

What clothing! O Lord my God, we worship
your clothes. Our God's a fashionable God;
no Presbyterian. New money. Not
a Catholic. Evangelical—furnished
with effective praise—no make-up except
will, lots of it, nothing but it, explaining
things to us inerrantly on the page—
a potentate to pagans. When the step-
son appeared we were rightly skeptical
and remain so. He was everything You
are not—visible in the dark, insolvent.
He walked, he loved, he ridiculed, he slept.
You tried to save him from his followers,
but there was nothing You could do.

Psalm 105

sing psalms unto him (a)

I'd like to have an audience of One—
but then again, I'm not so sure—who knows
aesthetics and appreciates a rhyme
that's just a hint in a rhythmic poem
even when the candy of its images
is metallic as blood, or when all you
get is visual assonance—ambiguity
be damned sometimes, when what the poem says
is all it says, as if Lord Tennyson
had eaten Eliot for breakfast, won—
an audience appreciative of form,
who sits up nights admiring human wit;
sly, kind, ironic, sad. [Here, warm applause
from the audience inside the poet.]

Psalm 105

> *sing psalms unto him* (b)

Unto whom else? Many of us have no
reader but the One who hears in secret:
"for I say unto you, when you pray, go
alone into your room and close your door;
the One who hears in secret will reward
you." On the busy streets no one will know
I was not good enough for anyone
but myself. (I planned to write "anyone
but God," but who could be that good or bad?
Is God who wants my poetry only
in my head?—He and I two kindly old
gents content, yea, pleased, with the mediocre;
one formerly in shorts—tan, grassy lad;
the other a Whirlwind of white and gold.)

Psalms for Skeptics

seek his face

Your face is home, and nothing else we have
is ours. The universe's filigree
of fire and colors and geometry
a billion billion deep is its own grave,
a vast performance of holes and splendor
perishing: an image always leaving
its mirror in our mind, magician's sleeve,
a shimmering house with its key next door
in Grampa's overalls pocket. He sits
at his little kitchen table, coffee
in an old cup warmed up from yesterday,
sugar cube a diamond die of snow, listening
to the radio, musing memories,
begetting you and everything he sees.

Psalm 106

they soon forgot his works

The supersized blue star Rigel, sixty
thousand times brighter than the sun, collapses
someday soon: its heated sacrifices—
the nitrogen of sons and daughters stripped
and spread across wide open spaces of waste—
will hollow out its core like a nation
sucking the blood of its poor. Thin marrow
sipped from their bones, they become dry shadows
circling to the bottom of a hand cupped
around a black and blood-stained hole—erupting
to a supernova—flambeau of gas
blue, white, red—wild excess!—its shredding flower
the settling shoulder of Orion's power.
Heed, ye heathen!—the heavy torch is passed.

Psalms for Skeptics

they murmured in their tents

They murmured in their tents, some centuries
before they were Jews—just Joe and Susie
Blow in the desert: something anybody
would have done—Arabs, campers, Comanches,
men, women. A tent is made for murmuring—
for a muffled, airy cinnamon breeze
under colored shade, warm afternoon peace—
made for murmuring and for being heard—
murmuring like water, murmuring like
a distant caravan, murmuring like
people lying looking up at the stars;
and who in the world do we think we are
to sleep under these stitches of glittering light?

Psalm 106

he is good

The Lord is good, and everything is one.
I can't believe Nels Mickleson is dead,
so set my memory of him—face red,
alive. What do I care for sunken bones,
stones, or all the comfort under the sun?
Lord, let me see him on his porch again—
the one on Ninth Street—but as he was then
and not in memory. Memory's done.
The heart's done. It's just a matter of time
and it will all be done—everything one:
one old stone in the cold—or in the mind
of Mr. Mickelson, the universe
drawing in like sand down the rounding course
of his life, in that chair, in the sublime.

Psalm 107

O give thanks unto the Lord

I've always pictured me as Grampa, sitting,
remembering, beneath the big old oak
out back—except that I would be more fit,
enough to walk downtown and cast a vote
for Lincoln come back joking from the dead.
I'd hear pretty good and still have my sight;
no hardening or hammer in my head.
"Half dead," he'd say; "but otherwise all right."
I'd take it with that quiet sense of humor
and know my Norsk without a dictionary;
and what he would assume, I would assume
peacefully, without that thousand-yard stare.
Whatever we were missing would be home.
Whatever he would wonder I would know.

Psalm 106

he is good

The Lord is good, and everything is one.
I can't believe Nels Mickleson is dead,
so set my memory of him—face red,
alive. What do I care for sunken bones,
stones, or all the comfort under the sun?
Lord, let me see him on his porch again—
the one on Ninth Street—but as he was then
and not in memory. Memory's done.
The heart's done. It's just a matter of time
and it will all be done—everything one:
one old stone in the cold—or in the mind
of Mr. Mickelson, the universe
drawing in like sand down the rounding course
of his life, in that chair, in the sublime.

Psalm 107

O give thanks unto the Lord

I've always pictured me as Grampa, sitting,
remembering, beneath the big old oak
out back—except that I would be more fit,
enough to walk downtown and cast a vote
for Lincoln come back joking from the dead.
I'd hear pretty good and still have my sight;
no hardening or hammer in my head.
"Half dead," he'd say; "but otherwise all right."
I'd take it with that quiet sense of humor
and know my Norsk without a dictionary;
and what he would assume, I would assume
peacefully, without that thousand-yard stare.
Whatever we were missing would be home.
Whatever he would wonder I would know.

Psalm 107

My heart won't let me live that long or see
that much. My two dry retinas are loose
already, tacked back down like parchment sewn
with scabby threads. I hear a dimming fizz
day and night. I have my first heart attack
under my belt and under my skin. Nights
aren't so good. I'm afraid of being sick.
If twenty years from now I'm still alive,
my teeth will be Chinese, I'll have steel knees,
and if I still can get around at all
I'll scuff from room to room reciting Keats
and urinating in my pants. My walker
will say "Kent." If beauty walks with Jesus,
someday soon the truth will walk with me.

Psalms for Skeptics

He brought them out of darkness and the shadow of death.

The light. "Move toward the light," they said. And then,
the name of Jesus on his lips, he breathed
his last. The lights and lines on the machines
unlit, and the last pressure left his hand.
The circle stood around his bed in light
they couldn't see, but they had heard the name
whispering through the crowd when Jesus came
healing, casting demons back into night,
telling the dead what they wanted to hear:
"Rise; come forth! I am the resurrection
and the Life." And then his mouth fell open;
they shuddered—one of them caressed his hair;
they wept. He looked at them, adjusted sight,
rose following the rumor toward the light.

Psalm 107

> *he satisfieth the longing soul*

The dead man rose—his spirit, that is, rose—
and regularly is in touch with us
through mediums, cats, and the garden hose,
though we are usually busy or obtuse;
but it's the thought that counts. Surely he thinks—
of us, I mean; or, well, of anything.
Does he need to think? What does he think with?
Does he ponder and discover his sins?
What are sins but despair, longing denied?—
and now he has his longing back, repaired,
the sins unnecessary, satisfied
like flowers with their water, light, and air;
like earth content with earth, and dust with dust.
Then what are we to him, or he to us?

Psalms for Skeptics

he brought them out of darkness and the shadow of death

Just leave her, Johnny, leave her—this soft ship
you won by birth: carpentered its green keel,
its twitchy rudder to its overweening
prow, rough-hewing it quick chip by quick chip,
stepping a mainmast shaped by other hands,
reefing sails to the wind's ghostly heartbeat,
working its veins and arteries like sheets—
and now the anchor drags and holds to land.
Step ashore and leave the corpse on the table,
the undertaker's forceps in her chest,
embalming fluid flooding her grey veins:
say goodbye, let her lie, and let her rest,
for not a hair nor heartbeat can be saved.
She brought you to the shore's forgiving breast.

Psalm 108

I will sing

My sonnet is a song of prayer—lament
and dismay at having to do without;
or wish-like vision "stricken-through with doubt;"
sometimes a moody new Jerusalem
of pagan sacrifice and praise, raw awe
and horror discordant, blaring like brass
and dental as gold in an out-held hand,
metered to pieces, obedient to law.
And sometimes the listener writes the lines,
composes the notes—and then I listen
more than complain. It isn't praise I hear;
it is my own heartbeat listening blind,
shuddering at the universal scare
and clawing the scales for intervals of air.

Psalm 109

> *They remember not to show mercy, but persecute the poor*
> *and needy, and even slay the broken in heart.*

The broken-hearted fill the earth like krill;
we feed on them, mouths wide as enterprise—
or else why would the desperate buy and buy?
We feed them diabetes and send our bill.
We have the law and profits on our side;
the churches of the dream are telecast
on screens the size of football fields. The last
Mohican signed his ballpoint x and died.
But let us give ourselves to prayer. The Lord
forgive us these our little sins; be pleased
to overlook the great: our blaspheming
the Holy Ghost, the infinitely poor,
whose universe was sold for the spare parts.
She broods and mourns. We're told it broke her heart.

Psalm 110

he shall judge among the heathen

The heathen went with Robert Kennedy
some distant place where being born again
is wise but doesn't matter worth a damn;
or they are marching to Montgomery
singing the old songs, walking hand in hand
with Bobby, Martin, Abraham, and John;
or they took the next bus for Birmingham
to see that insolently naïve swan
stagger on the cold wind, and try again.
Let us follow them to San Francisco
with flowers in our hair—one for children
born to marry the universal soldier,
one for the country I remember when,
and one for Jesus when he comes again.

Psalms for Skeptics

I'm writing now because there's nothing else
to do while waiting for that distant drum.
This is my way of going on a drunk
to change the world. The woman at the well
hallucinates under the midday sun.
She would have come early in the morning,
the doomed villagers shuffling and yawning,
but these days she prefers to come alone,
lowering the pail down that sunless hole;
until someone asks the smallest favor—
Water, just a little cup of water,
for the future, not for me, for the soul—
and the universal soldier's daughter,
quietly hoping this one's the Savior . . .

Psalm 111

the fear of the Lord is the beginning of wisdom

The "fear of God" required by the Torah is an *antidote* to religion.
— William Kilbrener, *Open-Minded Torah* (122)

The future in my pocket, stardust candy
wrapped in cellophane; God the Father slaving
for America; Christians being saved.
Flavor of the day: Brotherhood of Man.
Tomorrow—well, tomorrow is another day
so I will pray and praise Him while I can.
The hungry fear tomorrow and the poor
are squeezed so hard that centuries from now
they'll be a streak of oil miles underground:
but that is what the hungry poor are for.
"More light!" said Goethe, dying on his bed.
Now let us decompose, pulling Earth's blanket
over our small faces, shrinking and thankful
for a God our pagan fathers could invent.

Psalms for Skeptics

The pagan fathers, Presbyterians
at best, represented widely today
interdenominationally
and across all races, tribes, and nations,
meant well. They did not sacrifice children
lightly. They knew God—just as well as we;
they did not write scriptures sarcastically—
in fact, God wrote them. Where do we fit, then?
We are their water; their bones plow our bowels;
each Spring the same horse sheds his sand and stands
over our bed at night, his white eyes rolling,
and we cry for the same God. The world ends
anyway, the same way, before the same throne.
The fear of God is love of the unknown.

Psalm 111

I will praise the Lord with my whole heart.

The Old One surely wouldn't want such praise
as clatters from the clown kitchens of Earth.
The future is the whole of what we were,
so praise must be all the winking-out ways
we have abandoned—left at some altar
that even isotopes have forgotten,
a bushel of fireflies last night's boys caught
turning to earthy mush in a glass jar.
What of the Holy Bible speaks for God?—
the altars, offerings, the jealous rage?—
the widow's penny pressed by Caesar's steed
into the dust of the forgotten dead?—
hot miracles that lick up from the page?—
the crazy happiness of the blind saved?

Psalm 112

The desire of the wicked shall perish.

The wicked's brains will go right down the drains
much like everyone else's, I bet.
They'll all be on fire but their hottest desire
is just what the wicked won't get.
Lust strong and mighty will put on her nightie
and disappear into the night;
the Lord of the hood will commend the dead good
before He puts out the last light.
Is this what our Jesus was for?—to save
a concordance of ghosts? The rain falls the same
on the just and unjust, washing their laundry away.
The heavenly host will give up the most
forgetting, forgetting, forgetting all day
desires that were us, desires that are lost.

Psalm 112

Desire's the cycle of death and rebirth.
By the grace of God, the wicked will lose
their desire. The good are on their own. Suppose
that heaven is full of the wicked, pure
because purged, clean of the dreams of Earth,
innocent of memories, gold to the soul.
On Earth, they would be a parade of ghouls,
but in heaven they are feathered; they are birds.
The good must stay and suffer all things here—
herds of birth, skirts in every satan's snare,
earning the first curse by their lust to live;
having given all, scalded, fallen, scarred,
cheated by the power of the sweet hour of prayer;
these shall be with Jesus and remember who they are.

Psalms for Skeptics

trusting in the Lord

Let those who trust in God trust if they must—
but as for me and mine, we'll look out sharp.
Whatever can't be held by vigilance
is worthless. Take this matter of my heart
attack: should I eat pork and trust in God?
Or should I clot myself with globs of cheese
served over eggs. The best I ever had—
good Southern cooking, was tender beef bleeding
sour cream fried in bacon grease, white cheddar
grits cooked in whole milk—soft custard and fudge—
oh man. That roast couldn't have been redder
if it was roses. I just love that stuff.
 And this is what I got for trusting God:
 clogged arteries. You can't do what you want.

Psalm 112

The counter-argument is obvious:
What the hell? What are you talking about?
What does what you want have to do with trust?
What does cheddar cheese have to do with doubt?
For surely doubt is trust. If vigilance
is doubt, then let us man the battlements,
because there is no God to fall back on—
only the unknown lover in the chance.
If you can trust the Lord enough to doubt,
unafraid of a God of certainty,
unafraid of all but living without
the intimate within, then—but we'll see.
The angels give up faith for certainty—
or do they wonder, where we only see?

Psalms for Skeptics

The Lord can take away this suffering—
or so the Bible says. The praying pagans
of all ages have stayed awake for pay,
afraid to not pray, waiting for something:
and many are answered; there is no question.
This should not be. The Lord's Prayer said simply
for the Lord—a voice crying out dimly
articulate in a nightmare, the best
one can do in sleep—that should be just right.
Or why not pray for fun, just the sheer fun,
of careful, spider-like composition?
What can you get from listening at night
but the terror of horses on the road,
slowly walking, clop-clopping: growing old.

Psalm 112

To wait and listen while you die is prayer,
"trusting in the Lord." There are other prayers;
the others work sometimes and this one doesn't.
(Resigned indifference and tired despair
work. Demons work.) This one's the most unpleasant
until you die beforehand, before death:
until you trust like a stone. That should be
the best: God praying, the Holy Ghost's breath
breathing through me, me exactly nowhere
but here, attentive as a cup of tea.
The breath assumes a focus of the air—
each awake in the other, I and she—
awakening forever in the prayer,
the birth and circle of unending prayer.

Psalm 114

who humbleth himself

He suffered with us.
                              The Trajan statue
in Ankara still overbears; you look
up, and the face hardly looks down at you.
The muscular breastplate is a stone book
and you can't read it. You couldn't lift it.
This emperor could make Greek gods obey,
so did Rome mean power; so he became
a god indeed and is a god today:
a god is power in the very name.
Rome is stone on stone; its letters are stones
the size of capitols. Kneel, then go about
your business; make roads.
                                   When God was alone
under the Romans, reciting his doubt,
he died on his wood; we felt them lift it.

Psalm 114

Judah was his sanctuary

If God did go with them out of Egypt,
made a holy habitation in them—
but that is what the Germans call *verruekt,*
the *Gott mit uns* mistake that looks the same
from any victim's point of view—the Jews,'
the Poles,' the Canaanites,' the Mexicans';
but if, I say, their victim wasn't you,
you might believe it, and it would be news:
our Gentile God consorting with the Jews.
But they weren't Jewish yet. They were nothing
but slaves on the run under malediction,
old spirituals, old Negro psalms to sing,
mixing up like blood their facts and fictions,
arguing their way to crucifixion.

Psalms for Skeptics

Tremble, thou earth, at the presence of the Lord.

The Lord is not inside the iron core
of Earth, bubbling and spongy like crushed blood;
not in the soiled crystal of thunder clouds
drawing water up from our punished shores;
nor the hired mountains, these mighty purple
blah blah shifting wrinkles on the world's face;
nor in the rivers' everlasting race
into the relatively-speaking All
of oceans puny in cosmic warp and yaw;
nor is the Lord in the still small voice
of conscience, prophecy, of assembled
worshippers, of scriptures, properties, law,
or the rat-trap psychology of choice—
but in heaven-spent surrender. Tremble—

Psalm 114

What aileth thee, O thou sea . . . ?

What aileth thee, O sea; what sinks in you
like cold? What thin black fingers draw across
the reeds of your slackening longitudes
like fate? What do you vomit on your shores
like ink in glistening burls, your dull words
moaned thick from the pit of your poets' nightmares?
Do unfathomed dead mock digestion, hurled
from tide to tide with algae in their hair?
Surely you are greater than rotten men,
O sea—those bloated floats of flesh drooling
and defecating in their inventions
while the revolving moon makes you her fool
and the superstitious, globe-eyed squid
gulp globs of glutton-pumped oil like jugs of Id.

Psalm 115

Their idols are silver and gold, the work of men's hands.

Please, I need a sweet deal, want something real,
an automobile I can feel, steel wheels
that can peel—a treat for the street, secret
pet, a jet I can set and forget
but not yet: first I need a creed to believe
like jeans, better vespers, prayers that don't err
on the side of despair, matins that feed
and complines like wine, fat stats in the air—
more years, fewer tears, satin and money
like milk and like honey, thousands of bonds
and houses for blondes; nights soft, days sunny,
time to spend without end amen: then John's
God—Word made car, full of race and youth, big V-8,
all requests met. There will be silence while I wait.

Psalm 115

But our God is in the heavens

Our God is in the heavens and will not
come down; He rests between the blue steel pillars
of His airy battlements and will not
wake up, whether overgrown Romans kill
His own son, or you die, or generations
of confused Jews are put to death naked
as baby Job. Let's just see how gracious
He is if we kill a few kids and rape
their mothers. We can do whatever we want
and He'll stay there, up there, a Timbuktu
in the air. I wish it were different
but for that we have to uninvent Him.
So who's the Maker sitting next to you,
the one who goes wherever heaven sends him?

Psalm 116

What shall I render unto the Lord . . . ?

I have a lot to offer someone like
God, the God of Sunday morning's Power
Point, the God that requires the sweet hour
of prayer, the high God of Lucky Strike
and righteousness world without end, amen.
I've worked a lifetime on my resume
to stand on Judgment, or a rainy, Day.
I get embarrassed every now and then.
For once, perhaps, the taking's what I'll give—
the only thing I have—these open hands
given me by God. I'm a fisherman
at best, waiting for what I can't believe.
I will take and take and take, and again
take, and accept the cup of salvation.

Psalm 117

The truth of the Lord endureth forever. (Good Friday)

No matter that he dies a criminal
asphyxiated after being whipped
to strips of flesh with rusty nails and bits
of glass?—nailed right onto a wooden wall
of atheism, forsaken but not
fatherless—the father watching over
it all armed with legions of angels hovering
for the word—his mother watching all she's got
gasping to death looking down at her, cross
outspread for her like jaws of a black star.
Is this the eternal truth: it's all loss,
one thing after another 'til it's all
gone? If so, what the hell was it all for—
the love, the hope, the suffering eternal?

Psalm 118

> *Blessed is he that cometh in the name of the Lord.* (Holy Saturday)

"The holy one of God," the Nazarene
appeared to be—God down on earth among
us as much as God can be in a man—
healing green lepers, making the blind see.
Were we wrong? Surely this is an evil
day, a day of the dead, a day of God's
death, dead and buried, an absence colossal
in its presence—No God finally real
and undeniable. Only knowing
who God is do we know that God is done.
What a world—what a windy world, cold woe
blowing through space unknowing and unknown;
no heaven, no justice on a gold throne.
There is no Living God. We are alone.

Psalm 118

> *This is the day which the Lord hath made;*
> *we will rejoice and be glad in it.*   (Easter)

We came to say goodbye—goodbye to hope,
to wash its body of the last of earth
and leave it where it never could be hurt
again. What happened next is widely known:
the angel soldiers rolled away the stone
before us, and one still sat in the tomb.
His white robe glowed when he told us the news.
But the victory still belonged to Rome:
Jesus lives—we saw him later; he went
to heaven and into hearts, and he waits
for us, but Rome did get him off the streets.
He will not trouble Galilee again
or come home. Sweet pomegranates and dates
are ours alone, and we will wash the sheets.

Psalms for Skeptics

We'll never have him back the way he was.
Will no one understand that this gladness
aches? Heaven is not good enough for love;
we want the flesh for tenderness, caress—
for time, for miserable, passing time
on a summer shore beside the old lake—
the amused, the flashing look in his eyes
when a man stuck on stone legs ran away
terrified—the way he would say things clean
as could be. We have loved him, our Jesus.
Hope is gone now we know, we who believed
from the first, following our God-With-Us
to death, our dearest teacher and brother,
who gave us ourselves, gave us each other.

Psalm 119

Thy word have I hid in mine heart.

I sure hope it's there—my heart—Galilee
and you waiting. I'd like to go fishing
and you are invited; just you and me
or really just me, finally done with wishing,
and content—because I have a hunch
that anywhere you are, the whole damn world
is there, everybody sweating for bench
in my little rowboat. I'm getting old
faster than I am learning how to pray,
but I would like to know what Mary knew
when she was at the tomb—she thought alone—
and Jesus rolled away the cold unknown
around her name: she had nothing to say.
The Holy Ghost spoke, and it was you;
the Church sat down around her stone by stone.

Psalms for Skeptics

Open thou mine eyes

We've always been a thankful people here,
appreciating all the bounty loaded
on our forebears by an approving God:
the beautiful, ever-swallowed frontier—
the Cherokee were Philistines—and half
of Mexico cried out for a southern
border. It didn't cost us much trouble.
We have canned the land like a fatted calf.
The other nations have done worse than this
and dreamed no dreams. But a land of promise
must have a lot of promises to keep:
must have a lot of strangers to take in
to walk its alabaster cities' streets
and brush the chilly ghosts of Indians.

Psalm 119

We have no vision here; the prophets all
are dead. We are doing fine, but the people
perish. Who can see them?—they are so small.
Let's avoid the beginnings of evil
and plant a wall of gorgeous gardenias
white and rumpled like a writer's wastebasket,
each one a beautiful failed scripture, thus
abasing violence to mere bad taste,
transforming resentment into fragrance
like a groping jolt of opium, pious
by design like a white Mercedes-Benz,
God's comfort planted right between the eyes,
petals like page corners swirling around
a pollen-less center too pure for sound.

Psalms for Skeptics

Then let the poor lapse into desuetude,
unused as violets, bodily assumed
by the moon in June. What then shall we do?
Nothing! but sing. Isn't this the Good News?
At peace, at ease, in meditative quiet,
released like cool bees to our clammy cells,
buzzing our Ohms like sonnets gone riot,
electric with Nothing, with what the hell,
for we are nothing if not spirituelle.
So much for the kingdom of God on earth,
where angels work and the enlightened sing.
If I sing, I still sing under a curse—
that I am skeptical of everything—
poor words, poor words, old stones under the verse.

Psalm 119

If the poor are fed up with anything
it is with us. The will of God feeds them,
strange as it may seem, but it's in their dreams—
some violent, some peaceful as the rings
of Saturn, from this distance. That's God's way
of making universes: first darkness,
then dreams, then cherry pie with cream on top
and microbes in the water. All made up
like a prom queen and stuffed inside the ark
of orbit, Saturn strips for telescopes
and we beget wonder. Oh, we can pray
to wed her but we would have to elope—
impractical, hallucinatory.
Be content with dreams—the same old story.

Psalms for Skeptics

But God will find a way, they always say.
The way is us; what other way is there?
We are the law, and the law is the way
of all flesh. Because the Law is everywhere
and nowhere, we must have light to bind it—
laser-burned commandments engraved in air
by the hand that thought the Law and signed it,
necessary to make us slaves to sin,
wound around ourselves from ankle to chin—
a wilderness perfect to wander in,
a closed cranium oval as an egg,
with no-one to worship but everyone
home, the Temple carried on trembling legs—
reading from *aleph* the language of bones.

Psalm 119

A little vision is a dangerous
thing, because unless you can see it all
at once, the flower in the crannied wall
is natural, is merely one of us;
unless it grows to artifice, along
with prophecy and law and all the Psalms,
the past and future delicately wrought
like olives from the branch's perfect tongue—
and all is well in darkness and in light,
Maker eye to eye: but possessing verse
by verse is perception, the brain and eye,
many-armed Kali, image on image
destroying the unity of the worlds
line by line and flowering page by page.

Psalms for Skeptics

For oneness is not beyond the whole soul,
but within her. Meditating on Law,
the mind relaxes into one and all,
a sitar with a universal bowl—
and there comes another face, sapphire blue,
to measure forth the lotus of the soul
with singing, one song free and numerous
as gods, to which the whole creation moves
motionless as the soul of the lotus.
The Word has come to rest; the lamp within
opens outward like a flower. All things
visible and invisible begin.
The poor are satisfied with suffering;
the holy mountain crowns a shepherd king.

Psalm 119

their hearts are fat as grease

The "proud" have "hearts as fat as grease": disgusting,
but that is the only revenge you get
on those whose self-interest controls your fate—
a psalm, a prayer; no nut kicking, jaw busting,
tummy punching, and nothing from the courts.
The proud ruin history and get off
Scot-free. You can just turn your head and cough
if you don't like it. Prayer's the last resort,
but don't expect God to do what is just
to all those sons of bitches out there, happy
and unkosher as pigs in shit, too big
for their britches and way too big for us.
Their prayers are bird turds and they have crappy
inner lives, but there's no damn justice.

Psalms for Skeptics

"Their hearts are fat as grease"? Come on. They work
out. They don't eat refried beans and sour cream
like Mexicans. Their jobs are like sweet dreams:
no stress, no boss, no hard labor; all perks.
Their health insurance works better than prayer.
When they want a vacation, they take it;
when they want love like money, they make it.
Good teeth, good eyes, good faces, and good hair—
and need I mention clothes? Best of all: cars.
"Fat as grease" means satisfied, and they are.
Where is God in all this? On their side, they
say. And who can prove them wrong? Lazarus
wouldn't make it in the city these days;
his God is sleeping on the Third Street bus.

Psalm 119

And that is just the way it is, *muchachos*.
God is silent when we raise objections.
Consider, if you will, the Taj Mahal,
dying from her people's smoke injections,
a leper wrapped in rags of CO_2,
her once translucent rosy flesh chipping,
eaten slowly by green, uremic dew—
a chalky sputum on her tender lips.
Heart of my heart! You are yourself the tomb
of light, all the light I lived by. Krishna's
hands closed like the last night around a rose.
My path is the seven worlds of why,
my way the endless birth canal of sorrow,
and each direction in the world's a lie.

Psalms for Skeptics

Love is not an answer but a question,
a word in a dream, a way in water
walked by the heart on a sea of longing.
The heart was not made to sleep or to rest
but to seek, to need, to give everything
always, to mourn, to refuse all heavens
and wander the hills of birth forever.
Who has given us this heart? What longing,
what sadness no universe of blue fires
and no resurrections from Krishna's deaths
can satisfy, what infinite desire
in whose pure breast, from whose eternal breath
this heart, this lean and beaming eye, this light
upon my path, this way into the night?

Psalm 119

Thy word is a lamp unto my feet, and a light unto my path.

Thy nimble Word's a will-o'-the-wisp, here
and not here, a glimmer down the trail
that could be moonlight, the pines silver sails
in a sea of alcoholic thin air;
or is it a trail at all, this despair
so high and fine that it exhilarates
itself to trust, altitude in steep waves
with troughs so deep the ocean floor is bared?

One by one, the Word of God lives and dies
on the wind, and we believe what we can—
god after god worshipped and sacrificed
alive: a bull, a goddess, or a man—
what's laid in one tomb, bone and rags, will rise
in the next: the wheel comes around again.

Psalms for Skeptics

And light is light no matter what the sun.
The North Star dies in Ursa Minor, turns
into a sapphire charioteer, and burns
like duty in a new millennium.
Light of light and very God of very
God, begotten before all worlds were made—
utterly deniable in the shade;
ineluctable as the dictionary:
words, words, the way light suffers in its words—
the hidden poetry of absolutes,
the inarticulate disguise of truth,
the first command that no-one could have heard
but God wrapped in the oldest undertow
of night, then a path through the starry snow.

Psalm 119

Thy word is a lamp unto my feet, and a light unto my path.

Under the right light I have shapely feet
and I know my way around, but show me
the way to my name. Where is the old street
carpeted with palms?— maybe they know me
there. I watched from a window half asleep.
I heard the people murmuring early
but I was lazy, afraid to be seen
out there platinum, breathless, and girly,
with nothing on but my new radio.
I was a citizen of Rome, you know,
and Hollywood was such a jealous Joe.
So I prayed for my savior to go,
took a few pills, called JFK and lay
down naked and waited. Show me a way.

Psalm 120

Woe is me, that I sojourn in Mesech,
                    that I dwell in the tents of Kedar!

When all else fails, you pray. New Jersey looks
like up from here. The sewers are called schools,
and all the cops are evangelicals.
The criminals wear suits, the books are cooked,
the last honest pope left a year ago.
They sell lottery tickets and babies
in the churches. The dogs all have rabies.
Where's a guy get a drink? Nobody knows.
It's bad and it would be getting worse if
it could. They are illiterate as birds.
My hopes, my dreams, my words, are running sores;
I'm the only one who still prays in cursive.
I hereby call God down on my neighbors.
They're still mowing their lawns. What's prayer for
if it doesn't work?

Psalm 120

> *Woe is me, that I sojourn in Mesech,*
> *that I dwell in the tents of Kedar!*

My daughter is in Mesech now, somewhere
between the Black Sea and the Caspian.
There, muezzins call the faithful men to prayer;
their songs waver like poems. The women
dress like gardenias, beautiful secrets
whose children have gorgeous eyes and soft dreams.
Her apartment window looks toward the sea
across an infinity of small streets.
Her man sees everything, and together
they touch their words as Phidias touched gold.
When I am not dreaming, the world feels good
and wherever anyone goes it's heaven.
But Phidias knew nothing about wood,
how it warms to the hand, or how old
I am.

Psalm 121

> *I will lift mine eyes unto the hills. From whence cometh my help?*

It's all unthinkable—the millions killed
in brute-brained wars, a third of the world starving
ignored. "What is it that makes these hard hearts?"
Who unproves the suffering of children?
Then the cool, curt denial of your will—
the horror of your body in a grave.
It is no answer simply to be brave:
even the Savior labors up the last hill

and no-one answers when he recites "Why?"
No-one helps. What kind of answer would help?
Why should we hail anyone as we die,
whether to praise or to call down some grace?—
it's all the same. We will all lose ourselves
and everything else. Still we look, and wait.

Psalm 121

My help cometh from the Lord

I would have slipped and fallen through a crack
in my dreams; I would have lain like Adam
where I fell, bound and determined and damned
in a tomb hewn in black rock, no way back
to anything. But I awakened: this
gift comes from nowhere and no one but God.
What He has given, would He let elapse—
light's time up when this universe collapses?

We are of God; our light is the grand white
of being. Would this all fall through its own
hole unless God too surrendered? To what?
We are of God: there is nowhere to go
but awake; nothing is gone, and the first
dark stopped, never was, at the first Word's burst.
The soul of sight can't be folded in stone.

Psalms for Skeptics

The Lord is my keeper

He neither slumbers nor sleeps, the Old One,
and all the rest depends; and where it ends,
the Son of Man begins, the Begotten
Eternally, and with the Father, One—
"begotten, not made"—figure in the stone
before the stone was made: the sculptor wakes
and the figure comes to light: artist makes
whatever the maker made: three in one.

I was asleep, a pebble in the hand,
curled like a pearl, like a kernel's tight germ,
a stone. Alone, for sleep is circular
as a world. But God is alive in the bone
of the bowl of the awakening poem,
oh my soul that is the rose of His hand.

Psalm 121

My help is in the name of the Lord

How'd you like some ornithologist
to name you Junco, Titmouse (Tufted or
Just Plain)?—so you would have to swallow with
your own name, a virtual cuspidor
on the spat floor of the Last Chance Saloon,
which is Life. You could be named Floyd instead
of Evan, Welsh instead of Anglo-Saxon;
or Belgian, like Cosmo. For every royal Fred
there are a hundred Mortimers and Jacks on
the dole waiting for their daily payout
of ridicule. A name is a buffoon
waiting for the cue to fall on its face
in the next age. Stay away from names. Pray
to a place on the dark side of the moon.

Psalms for Skeptics

My help is in the name of the Lord

The name of God is greater than a name
as light is greater than the sun. "I Am"
is a refusal to be named; the flame
consumes the understanding of the man,
and not the bush. The visual leaves and wood
are music in that light, more heard than seen,
but the still voice cannot be understood
until its clean syllables are eaten
like manna in the wilderness, the food
of angels. Our peculiar appetites
become our signature, what's understood,
our leather tent, our beggar's cups of eyes.
The Holy Name made the hot universe,
and all it wants is oxygen to burn.

Psalm 121

The Lord shall preserve thee from all evil

May God preserve me from everything but
myself, by which I mean the Royal Self
whose kingship is in God alone, and not
the servant self whose head is dressed in Ralph

Lauren and Hollywood, who needs new cars
to get to heaven, one for each mythic
mile, and who goes off to the latest war
like a sport—him, no. I'm sympathetic

to him, but he scares the hell out of me.
When he bleeds, I think I am going to die;
he makes a mistake and it's tragedy,
as Aristotle says. He's made of lies,

but some are good lies and they serve him well.
He doesn't know me; only knows himself.

Psalm 122

> *I was glad when they said unto me,*
> *Let us go into the house of the Lord.*

The church where I grew up smelled like a church should smell,
the solid woodwork painted Lutheran white exactly right
for God; and every Sunday morning it was light
and beautiful outside and in. Here God would dwell,
if anywhere on earth. The Pastor would perspire
alone—preaching with his fists and military
crew cut, for he had prayed the crew to Hiroshima;
an eye askew—the rest of us were clean and dry.

The man knew sin like wolves know deer. Sometimes he grinned
as if to eat us up, and blow to sticks the house
he'd built for God, leaving just the pulpit and him
after that holy and consuming flash went out—
a wilderness of churchlets empty, ashen, black,
all evangelical. I wish we could go back.

Psalm 122

Our feet shall stand within thy gates, O Jerusalem

Our feet shall stand within thy gates, when feet
are left behind; our hands shall touch thy walls,
when hands lie on our hearts; and we shall see
the gold in the temple, when eyes are gone,
Jerusalem, thou city of the dead.
The Living God shall make thee with His mind,
and all His dead shall walk thy streets again
amazed. What absolute, new stars shall shine
from thy sky, and what resurrected sun—
that we could recognize? Low satin walls
secure thee, and the locks upon thy gates
are fastened down; the penitential psalms
are chanted softly and thy priests are grave.
How fixed the light of that late-dawning sun—
understanding when understanding's gone.

Psalm 123

Have mercy upon us, O Lord, have mercy upon us.

My other life came to its end today
and left me here with this. Until today
I thought this was pretend, imaginary
as the cattle of the sun, an image
of a dream Ulysses dreamed enchanted—
watery, wavery ladies chanting
the nursery songs of the gods: another
chance somehow hidden in the lyric, other
people to be born with, other castles
to gaze upon like heroes, some other cast
to play the same Shakespeare; but this is life
and only this one faltered speech is life.
There will be no other for the wanderer
on these boards, no other wood. One Wanderer.

Psalm 123

What we have left unlived was beautiful.
Angelic was the stained glass blue of love
that flooded heaven's steady canticle
of what might have been, should have been, what was
conceived in God's allowance, God's power;
holy the hands that carried from table
to mouth that slow, sweet communion of ours;
blessed by the storm of creation's first rage
the longing in our single heart for God.
Instead we wrestled the angel of God
like a poet fighting rhyme, building image
after image of the gritty curtain
of desire, the falling absence of Him
who pushed us free. Have mercy, have mercy.

Psalms for Skeptics

For we have murdered universes,
and now what always was can never be
because of us. How still the birds in trees
beyond our comfortable circumferences,
how interesting the questions posing
like shadows against the outsides of our
walls! Creatures walk in beauty at this hour
unnoticed and mindless as steam. We chose.

But how were we to know? How could we not?
You can see the writing on the wind sometimes,
and pleasure is a garden by the sea
where the lost all come to light, and mere thought
redeems the winding serpents of the mind:
all is possible again in beauty.

Psalm 124

they had swallowed us up quick

Had not the Lord been on our side, subjunctive
mood had been extinct, present tense exclusive
now, and poets speculative—reclusive
in the best of times—had been long since defunct.
But God is our right hand. Let those who swallow
swallow this: iussive, hortatory,
circumstantial, causal. End of story.
Without imagination nothing follows
darkness, chaos, Elder Night. Had not God
spoken what was then contrary to fact,
without form and void, interrogative
(why not?) perhaps, perpussive, very loud,
and making circumstantial what could live
only if uttered, there would be no acts.

Psalms for Skeptics

Our soul is escaped

How hard it must be for the dead to do
without their children in the Bye and Bye.
For grief, no salty tears to cry:
no eyes! You miss them, but there's nothing you
can do. How nice to be with your old Mom
and Dad, your fishing pals, queer old Uncle Earl.
But what about your little baby girl;
the boy you threw the football with? What's home
without them? The cutest grandchild in the world
can't bring you back from that Serene Embrace,
release or loosen the Eternal Now.
How can I visit you without a face,
you children clinging to the golden bough,
the first fruits of an everlasting race?

Psalm 124

Our help is in the name of the Lord

The doctrines simplify, and lose their words
to prayer. Systematics: thy kingdom come—
theodicy: thy will be done on earth—
eschatology: hallowed be thy name.
I pant for Trinities like water brooks;
my shepherd is the Incarnation seen.
The Law and Prophets and the holy books,
the disciplines of all the sects: Amen.
Teach us to pray, that I may see thy face
and dwell in the house of the Lord forever—
prayer as wordless as the evening leaves,
understanding as the summer river
beside green trees, the beautiful words slow,
and falling, and going where the wind goes.

Psalms for Skeptics

> Let us say prayer is poetry observed,
> attention to the all-creating Word.
>
> Our help is like the river and the leaves,
> breath of the Eternal in old countries
>
> where the streets smell of cooking and old clothes,
> wisdom somewhere, but where, nobody knows.
>
> The sun goes down there a sharp and smoky red,
> and prayers for peace might as well be unsaid
>
> for all they do, and the poor have large eyes
> and are slow yet somehow children survive,
>
> and old men thin as trash manage to smoke.
> They wait; they've always known that they are old.
>
> This is the City of God. Those who wait
> here like to watch from the easternmost gate.

Psalm 125

Do good, O Lord, unto those that be good

If beauty is its own reward, then God
does good in everything and all is well;
the good are beautiful. Do what we ought,
and they can keep their doctrine of the Fall;
be true in all our inward parts and give
our gladness to the poor, no Grand Inquisitor
can take from us the certainty we have
in feeling what we feel. There's Lipitor
for hardness of the heart, there's Prozac
for the bends; studies show that meditation
works. Let the sick take care of the sick.
Let us let the nay-sayers say their nays,
for blessed are they that mourn, and blessed the poor.
There is peace, and peace, and peace everywhere.

Psalms for Skeptics

And everything is one. Selfishness
is delusion for swimming senses' sakes.
The bird that dips the Galilean lake
quiets the mind, the pain of fibered sense,
with the transparent, gem-pure, solid pearl
it drops into the sacred diadem
of understanding. David's Bethlehem
unfolds its lotus on a watery world.
The Beauty of the Lord is everywhere:
the universe assumes its drops of praise
as a pearl assumes the sea, a round prayer
tighter than a mustard seed, and the flares
of supernovae sow the softened waves
like words across the Galilean page.

Psalm 125

the Lord is round about his people

The circle is unbroken, now and always:
beauty is the Way from energy
to matter, back to thought, and round again
to energy, with all the uncreated
space surrounded like the Mediterranean
Sea. The Holy Spirit forever bends
her wings of light around an empty nest.
From nothingness we come in wild surmise;
under that beating heart as wildly die,
comforted by that uncreated breast.
The beauty of it is the only thing—
heaven says it—beauty is never lost—
circumference of the whole celestial host—
mathematics—apples—a sudden ring.

Psalms for Skeptics

The explanation of it all is shattering.
Who knows anything? Where is the hope in it all?
What's the good of being one Transparent Eyeball,
or the sound of warm rain endlessly pattering,
or the touch of a hand upon another hand?
Let us all be absorbed and grow like cheese—
a gold, inevitable, holy wheel—
an awesome gift for the first mouse that understands
physics. Why not? The booming cosmos is its own
meaning, dust and billions of little brains neither
adding to nor subtracting from the grand total.
Let us render unto Caesar what is Caesar's.
Let us breathe and pray and practice Yoga
until hell freezes over, or we see Jesus.

Psalm 126

we were like them that dream

We woke, "and found the dream was true": Beauty
is the truth in spite of everything we
see with the eyes of desire, attachment
to results of what we do webbing us
to pain of *Maya*—the magical rent
in sight that makes us see what never was.
Oh, which is dream—the prestidigitation
or the hand, the insight or the desire,
the union with all things or the raw fire
of murder and starvation? Who can say;
without a fulcrum who can move the Earth?
Each is a dream, from the other shore.
Beauty is a river, itself the more
it changes, endless curve of death and birth.

Psalm 127

Unless the Lord build the house, they labor in vain that build it:
except the Lord keep the city, the watchman waketh but in vain.

Unless He build the house; except He keep
the city. . . . Does He turn His back on those
He doesn't build or keep? Must we suppose
instead an alien work of God, a deep
game played by the left hand, a will that breaches
walls around the innocent for the long
plan? Or worse, could God's hand expose the wrong
man? Surely the death of Jesus teaches
something. But what? That God can turn from God
and still or even more be God? Unless
the Lord give answer, they labor in vain
that question. The crucifixion's a hard
answer, a premonition—the distress
before a heart attack, then dreadful pain.

Psalm 127

In the deep fen country, down in the dark
peat, black holes are long ships. Their travelers
skeletons in rotten leather, banded iron
helmets masking missing eyes, they ride their arks
from dark to dark, gilded with grim gods
on gold shields, sword hilts jeweled in blue
and red like battle in stars, dew of new light
beamed in blood of dying giants; courage, murder,
earls of lightless worlds stroking the old blows
as the raven river flows—sent by their dead
gods somewhere and still going, ghosts in bones
from unknown to unknown. The sky a starry sod,
we lie, horrors on boards, learning the Lord
who builds, who watches, who slaughters the gods.

Psalm 128

> *Blessed is every one that feareth the Lord; that walketh in his ways . . . happy shalt thou be, and it shall be well with thee.*

The world's a stone; it's one big rolling stone
as final as a stopper on a tomb:
what starts here ends here, and we are alone.
It's birth and death and nothing else, and soon
we'll shoot, pollute, and not reboot our home.
A stone! A stone! My kingdom is a stone,
and stone on stone my universe has grown,
a tomb where distances are thicknesses
of walls, and time is depth beneath a sea
of light I cannot see. Truths became guesses
long ago, when I found that I can read
in this dark. The shroud will never be sewn
that can reach me here. With the Lord I can
walk out. I feel in the stone for his hand.

Psalm 128

I worship the walls of my circumference.
Someone, perhaps I, have painted numbers,
figures, words like Neolithic horses,
running figures—wild beasts and hunting men,
gods before which I bow, kneel, and humble
myself; women. I touch paint. The walls bleed.
The ceiling reels with stars in their courses.
The floor heaves like a molten iron sea:
upon it I lay the skull of my head
where the Outside comes clothed in woven dreams
draping its unimaginable light.
Out there is the land of the withered dead:
they have nothing. Here we have our old night,
ancient drawings that almost seem to move,
quiet comfort of happy, happy love,
the chase, maidens, sacrifice, painted light.

Psalms for Skeptics

But now the painted windows of desire
are closing; the tinctured stars turn to rust
from iron-bloodied water; a stone lust
creeps on the floor; the walls' ancient eyes
have gone out. Hard circumference closes in.
There is no denying it: we will die.
The tomb will dry up like dew. A hand print
on a wall will reveal the facing hand
in a horrid miracle of surprise,
and the walls, thin as paint, will become glass.
This is not prophecy: the world will turn
to fact. Our image on the glossy walls
lies down and with a groan the stone gears roll
apart. Everything will burn. Desire burns.

Psalm 128

And then all will be well, sweet to the root,
the last mad witch drawn back into the trees,
and all suffering refined to beauty.
There will be no lovers; there will be no dreams.

The stone has been rolled away like a boy's hoop
in a nineteenth century painting come
to life, and the long thoughts of a lost youth
will lead the last distrustful poet home.

Adam will awake to find his dream true,
as if nothing had happened, no lost Keats
to weep, for the lost walk in beauty
at last, and what was dreamed at best will be.

And God, who will God be on the first day?
Who is love, who is happiness, who is
the day?

Psalm 129

> *Many a time have they afflicted me from my youth . . . .*
> *the plowers plowed upon my back*

"Don't let the bastards get you down," he'd say.
The bastards always slapped him down. The plowers
shoved his face to the slop and plowed away,
glad to be principalities and powers.
Like Faust, this son of man had history,
the law, and worst of all theology.
A disappointed Mephistopheles
in spite had cursed him with longevity
and walked away whistling (sheer bravado).
The doctors made mistakes and blinded him;
his memory wore out. What would God do
in a similarly flat position?
  "All you've ever had is what you've got now,"
he'd say. "Don't let the bastards get you down."

Psalm 129

He had a wife; let's say the wife had him.
Materialized, a smiling Satan
in the black of a Presbyterian
kept him from falling into happy sins.
Oh, to be delivered from temptation
by the devil: what a desolation.
But hewing to a firm, deliberate path
(what path it was he didn't like to know),
he made his way; let's say the way made him;
but it was straight, and as the grave, narrow.
Demons would fall silent and watch him pass,
nervous with their hands and chewing their tongues:
the fear of God would stupefy their wrath
when they saw His blind and forsaken son.

Psalms for Skeptics

He had nothing at the end. One by one
the eyes, the dreams, the mind, and then at last
the body—a poem, its wrap of rhyme
undone to the structure, taken apart
by the beats, iambics unhammered,
the stitches of images unthreaded;
hollowed, unrounded, of the green glass bowl
of its form, back to the chatter of sounds,
the ambient earth syllabic as dirt.
Heaven open your gates to him; say light
to him in singing psalms as real as leaves;
take him in your sacred hands, cherubim,
you who stand in the presence of God; grieve;
carefully to the tender throne, bear him.

Psalm 130

Out of the depths have I cried unto thee, O Lord

They want me dead. My children want me dead.
This morning, Saturday, they will kill me.
They are so cold about it, decided:
this morning they will feed me my last meal
and take care of what needs to be done.
I don't know when they talked about it.
My absent daughter, "Goes her heart with this?"
I ask like Lear. They quote her cool message:
"Dear, dear," she wrote; that's all. Nobody cries.
Dead and buried in the ground. Why? They know.
They won't let me leave, won't let me go home.
Now, my last morning, hour. I put my
liver-spotted hand to the grassy cup.
I pray to Jesus and he wakes me up.

Psalms for Skeptics

Out of the depths

Out of the depths I cry to you, O Lord,
for those a little better off than I
in the long run: the children of the world,
the sly retirees with a poisoned eye,
the slang bangers who pray to strangers, angels
in out of the way cafes arranging
sales of second-rate indulgences,
old politicians trying to be brave
and failing in view of retirement needs,
businessmen in Bangkok looking for girls
and girls looking for a good guy like me,
poets looking for a break. Milton Berle
telling jokes in a sober heaven knows
what I mean, notes in the folds of his robe.

Psalm 130

Out of the depths

Out of the depths I cry, my little self
absorbed by medications marching single
file in my brain like Ringling Brothers elephants
walking a tightrope overhead, jungle
animals in paper cages obeying
prescriptions sent down on folded airplanes
by the audience, or clowns piling out
of cars as if justified by surprise
and then getting their painted fake heads shot
off—by the colorful little goodbyes
wrapped up in the meds, several in a cup,
as gaily motley as the barker's suit,
 who any minute now will send us home
 and say the Greatest Show on Earth is over.

Psalms for Skeptics

While we're at it, let's talk about elephants.
I have seen him. You have no idea
how big he is up close. Seeing's believing.
He shatters all seven seals when he pants
like a bellows. When he raises one foot
you see your face on it—your face and all
the rivets in Achilles' shield. Bugle?
Blue heaven folds together at that note.
He doesn't ask for your beliefs; he doesn't
talk. Call him "Simba;" see how far you get
with that. Crack the whip of your will—poor will.
He is streaked with mud and covered with dust—
drops the heavy Jupiter of his head
and lifts you with his trunk. Lesser gods kill.

Psalm 130

But there is forgiveness with thee, that thou mayest be feared.

Advent again—a year of life given,
gone past, a year of prayer with these Psalms
and little done to learn the gentle laws
of stone—or learn the latitudes of heaven.
My prayer is that this year may be forgiven,
things come right even though I know they're wrong,
that all this stuff is not counted at all—
the garbage I collect when I should be living.

Thank you for the year. The life has been lovely
however carelessly I have spent it,
fearful, selfish—but hasn't it been grand
to come around this way again?—above
the ground, laughingly and ignorant
of which is coming—the left or right hand—

Psalms for Skeptics

I wait for the Lord

I wait because I don't believe there is
an alien behind the alien
work—the left hand—of God. Sorrowful Friend,
Godot, every winter we wait again
for you; terrible bells carol; stiff trees
bleed for you; here is the gift of our knees.
We keep Christmas, as they used to do then.
What will you give me? Who will forgive me?

We keep Christmas like Tiny Tim—never
let him grow up whole, though we know he will,
and the miser pays the bills, happy to be here—
happy to surprise us, happy just to be.
The myth saucers down the hill for a spill.
What will you give me? Will you forgive me?

Psalm 130

> *My soul waiteth for the Lord more than they that watch*
> *for the morning; I say, more than they that watch*
> *for the morning.*

My sisters wait in Babylon for Israel.
A world away, the City of Angels
shoots the moon—its existence a gamble
that will pay off some sunny day in hell
if at all. I call my sisters Mercy
but they never call me back: I don't know
who I am. The world is waiting for me
but one day it will get fed up and blow.

Here in the church I cower in the pew
and sniff the fresh cut cedar in the dark,
thinking of my sisters and the worlds; few
enough of each there are. I feel someone
else is here, or about to be—an ark
beneath each foot, in every hand a gun.

Psalms for Skeptics

> *Let Israel hope in the Lord: for with the Lord there is mercy,*
> *and with him is plenteous redemption.* (Advent)

Would we believe, even if someone came
back from the dead—like pale Alcestis, either
Lazarus, or a skeptic neurosurgeon
whose neocortex-erased brain
flatlined seven days?—saying everything
is light, everything is love, everything
is God, and our iniquities—the world's—
transpare in the dawn of Eternity.

He comes back saying all is well, everything
is well, all manner of things—and like the *zhlub*
I say, "So can you prove it?—can you take
me there and show me this east-rising Ring,
this ocean more gold than Homer, penumbra
behind the mild surmise on your blind face?"

Psalm 130

And he shall redeem Israel from all his iniquities.   (Advent)

Don't do a thing except prepare the way
as best you can, O Israel, my alter-
ego, my savage, sacred *nebekh*; however,
He must know that we'll botch the job. The way
that is the Way is not the Way, the *Tao
te Ching* reminds us, re-enforcing Nordic
indecisiveness in *nebekhim* born
to doubt, like me. He knows the Way to go—

in fact He *is* the Way. The Redeemer's
way is paved with hallelujahs of sin;
praise, a festival of imperfection,
is brittle like glass and like glass it blurs.
The elders sense it, sitting by the gate.
The best thing anyone can do is wait.

Psalm 131

> *Let Israel hope in the Lord henceforth and forever.* (KJV)
> *O Israel, wait for the Lord*
> *now and forever.* (Tanakh)

That doesn't sound so good. "Wait forever."
What's another several thousand years
compared to waiting past the last cold star.
And "hope forever" doesn't sound much better.
Let's wait until we die; then let the next
waiter take over. *My name's Israel;*
I'll be your server tonight. Our specials
are salt and bitter herbs, as always. Check?
Never. Since you, the angels of the Lord,
aren't going anywhere until the end
of time, please rest your terrible swift swords
against the wall. Yes, under the writing.
The fingerpainted text glows until time bends
down to space and comes up lightning.

Psalm 132

I will satisfy the poor with bread

The poor—the poor—the everlasting poor
who wait for God: what is Zion to them?
You can starve as well in Jerusalem
as in New York City—another New
Jerusalem, as disappointment goes.
God can be absent anywhere. Starvation
is never out of place among our race.
We are alone anywhere the wind blows.

Let kings and wise men follow moving stars
and wear their visionary diamond time
like Rolex watches; let the mooing poor
bear witness like our blue Mother Mary
birthing the bloody news; let us adore
whatever baby haloes when God cries.

Psalms for Skeptics

The Babe awakes and god has left his heaven;
the angels sing—angels are always singing
in that sphere where what looks to us like wings
is music—and they know that all is well.
But Mary knows all too well that when God
comes here, He draws the empyrean down
like a blind. Philosophers are alone
with stuntmen, glittering strippers, Hollywood
detectives with perspectives like chopsticks;
and they know better than to complain. What
good would it do? Complain to whom? Right now
the Lord is learning his Aramaic
and hoping against hope to make the cut
with Joseph's hand on his over the saw.

Psalm 132

here will I dwell

As now we welcome Jesus to his world—
sweet world of dancing barefoot on the sand
that slides down shrinking circles
of time, sweet world of holding hands
on satin beds, of lilac and goodbyes,
of Easter lilies and one good Resurrection—
bridge to everlasting love, bridge of sighs—
are all of us murderers of heaven?—
or saviors? Evil not in him, in us—
what kind of world is this; what rounded thing
is our sweet freedom, latitudes of dust
that trap God, allowing us what? "Great Ring
of pure and endless Light," like a baby
unswaddled waving the angels away!

Psalms for Skeptics

Lord, remember David, and all his afflictions

The king, Great King, to fugitive reduced,
a whisperer in caves, soaking in clothes
he hasn't changed for weeks, his sword an old
rake with chewed edges, his small shield once used
by a fled general: did he, like Bruce,
see inspiration on a cave's cold stone—
a noiseless, patient spider throwing ropes
of filament for the King of the Jews
to hold, gossamer prayers—*Eloi,* why
have you forsaken all of us? Do Lord,
oh do Lord, do remember me, for I
am a Son of David, and I was born
to trouble as the sparks fly upward!
Like a mortal prayed; like a mortal heard.

Psalm 132

I have ordained a lamp for mine anointed.

Thy word shall be a lamp, but your Anointed
is the Word, and Light from the Light you are—
"the love that moves the sun and all the stars"—
heaven come to earth as a baby boy:
is this your way of saying he's on his own?
Will he die here, and never get back home?
The ox and ass, one dumb, the other dumber,
beat time but there's no distant drummer,
only Satan, who has got our number,
and the smartness in our brilliant phones.
The Magi come along to rumble,
carrying Luther in a burlap bundle,
a kicking sack they dump onto the stable floor,
bow low, and beat it out the open door.

Psalm 133

life forevermore

—is made for those who dwell in unity,
according to this Psalm, for unity
is like the dew, etcetera. This poem
ties eternal life to downright earthy
images, like the Belle of Amherst rowing
in Eden, or Whitman sewing his birthday
suit—just what you might expect from the Old
Testament's Leonard Cohens. Another earth
but touchier and feelier, body
barefoot on the cool dew of Hermon,
sunlight breezy in your now-perfect hair;
and the lover of your dreams on your breast
at night, breathing without the need for air,
the two of you just you, one and at rest?

Psalm 134

The Lord that made heaven and earth bless thee out of Zion.

Zion, Zion, all you hear about is Zion: Zion
this, Zion that. Old men sit at the gates
of Zion—watch the rising, setting sun
as it arcs over Zion, with its face
always upon Zion; and all the kings
on earth have their faces set on Zion—
want to capture it, wish they could bring it
back to Babylon or Iowa City,
wish they had a god like the God of Zion,
wish they had a harem of girls as pretty
as the uptown girls of Solomon;
and even Jesus had to turn his face
toward the avenues of Jerusalem
to die of grace forsaken, to be raised.

Psalms for Skeptics

Jerusalem, Jerusalem, you stone
the prophets, call the violent to prayer
in stolen robes upon your temples' stairs,
sell the poor to Christians for their bones—
oh how the doves fly upward from the market
tables, lambs bleat braised upon the altars,
while Jesus teaches with his lash of cords
the terrible deliverance of the Lord!
In you the procurator makes his bet,
the garden withers under blood and salt;
down falls on you the emperor's decree—
and you sun yourself like a Sheban jewel,
cerulean diamond fire, beautiful
upon the mountain, beautiful to see.

Psalm 135

> *The idols of the heathen are silver and gold,*
> *the work of men's hands....*
> *They that make them are like unto them:*
> *so is every one that trusteth in them.*

I feel myself becoming monofilament,
or like unto it, for I trust in it
to make me happy—of course to catch fish,
but mainly to keep me alive by the thrill of it.
By March I am so thirsty for a lake
that when I get there you'd think I could drink her
and in I go—hook, plastic lure, and sinker,
not caring if I slip the spool or break.

        They also serve who only stand and wait,
but I prefer to fish from boats, seated
with beer and sandwiches and an old friend.
I'm getting translucent and should cut bait,
but I trust bass more than I trust Jesus,
unspooling forever, line without end. Amen.

Psalm 136

his mercy endureth forever

What happens to forgiven sins—the ones
committed unto me for rumination
and loss of sleep? The sins will be expunged
from his/her account, but what about my rage?
The thief will sing hosannas with the angels
and I'll still be short fifty thousand bucks.
What do I get for ulcers and chest pain
besides enlightenment? The injured must
forgive, like God, who's robbed of being God
with every jot and tittle that we hold
out for—which is to be owed a whole lot
that can't be repaid. "See my servant Job,"
God says later. "He gets another wife,
more sessions on the Wheel, another life."

Psalm 136

Where is Job now, I wonder. Does his new
family cheer him up, come holidays,
or do the old ones who were blown away,
sons and daughters—not to mention goats, ewes,
cattle—materialize at Thanksgiving,
stay through Hanukah and Christmas?—a problem
for Zen-like, progressing Dad, who says God
killed them, not his own neglect. What a ribbing
we'd give him! "Gee, Pop; then who is to blame,
and how do we get over acts of God?"
It's always uncomfortable when we see
God, who used us as poker chips, with freedom
as our compensation. Have we learned? We
can do no wrong and no one is to blame.

Psalms for Skeptics

You see the difficulty with God's mercy:
it doesn't work without our help, and we
don't need it any more when we've let go.
What is it?—as intangible as light.
We get our freedom as we use it right.
That's a problem, too: there's nothing to know.
The mind's a very full and busy place,
but the Understanding—you can look through
it. Seen by the born, ever-marching you
it is nothing, a void, sheer empty space—
like looking at the wind to see one's face.
What if we are made of understanding?—
if everything that's made is made of grace.
Where's the justice, the law? Where is God's hand?

Psalm 136

It's all the law. The law is everywhere. Every
jot and tittle of the law shall be fulfilled,
for everything is grace, everything forgiven;
the only place is the Kingdom of Heaven.

                And here sits Brother Job, surrounded by
the charred and broken corpses of his children.
"You nebbish!" says his wife. "Curse God and die."
"*Om*," he answers. "I have painful boils. Still."
"All the more reason," she says. "Ashes, dust,"
he says; "naked came I. The whole *schtick*. But
does it help? No more than your shrewishness."
"Am I God? Can I watch you suffer and not scold?"
"The Lord has His complaints too, God knows.
So could it hurt, a little Jewishness?"

Psalms for Skeptics

Would it be too much to ask, a little love?
Job says to himself, filling out a form
to become a Jew. In the Land of Uz
a vague Protestantism is the norm
but Job has had it with being a gentile.
The Joys of Yiddish sits next to the shard
he uses to scrape the worst of his boils.
"*Nu*," he nods; "Buddhism says life is hard."
"So what's new?" the Mrs. asks. "Why not move
in with my cousin in America?
Life's easy there. God has nothing to do
with America. We could be chosen
without being Jewish." "*Nu*," he says again;
"God would understand if he had children."

Psalm 136

"We're all God's children," Job's wife reminds him;
"a lot of good it does." "Do you think," Job
muses, "—do you think He exists, our God?"
"Of course. Where else would all this pain come from?"
"We must accept," Job says with a bowed head,
"both evil and good from Jehovah's hand."
"Why should we? For once stand up like a man
and curse, so maybe He will strike you dead
finally. You sit there in your own pus
and expect to advance spiritually."
"There's no other way to advance in Uz."
"Invent something. For starters, something septic."
"I'll seek the Lord with all my heart and soul."
"What's to seek? You have the soul of a skeptic."

Psalms for Skeptics

Then the whirlwind came and Job was answered—
with questions, naturally; rhetorical
in nature, and very pointed. Thus all
his puzzles were solved—or so we have heard.
Of course none of this ever really happened:
it's literature, the Book of Job, no more.
Nevertheless, don't you kind of wonder
whether the Jobs moved to Los Angeles,
and whether he was answered—or enlightened?
Because as he stood there in the whirlwind,
his robes blowing and sand stinging his face,
how could Job do anything but look down
or hear any supernatural sound
until the dust fell, and the Ghost rose away?

Psalm 137

> *By the rivers of Babylon, there we sat down,*
> *yea, we wept, when we remembered Zion.*

The words are lovely but the water's deep.
Where do they end—the words and the water?
I can go without poems, do without,
and this new prayer can go without me.
No. Who can dream and do without his home?
You get careless after a while, throw things
into the wind as though they still had wings,
and in Babylon I grow old alone.
When the stars were born, Jerusalem, you
named them like children—like your own children
come up out of Egypts of sweat and sorrow.
Kings bowed at your tall gates, and I did, too—
when I was a young man, full of prayers—then—
who now measures words in small cups he borrows.

Psalms for Skeptics

> *By the rivers of Babylon, there we sat down,*
> *yea, we wept . . .*

Those rivers are sewers, as you should know;
and while suicide might sound exquisite—
your guitar leaning against a willow,
near the water a pile of linen clothes
scented lightly of lemon verbena—
you'd be filthier than hyena spit
when they pull you out. Not *aqua fina*
by a long shot; you have to hold your nose
when you take a leak. The ponds are as bad.
So anyway, if you're depressed, stay home
and pour yourself some Comfort, go to bed,
and don't worry: tomorrow will be worse.
Write a poem and end it with a curse
if it makes you feel better. Whatever works.

Psalm 137

> *Happy shall be he, that taketh and dasheth thy little ones*
> *against the stones.*

The only thing we have to pray is prayer
itself. These songs composed of selfishness
may cry or intercede, may curse or bless:
they're all culled from the roundabout of care
known as the Wheel of Birth and Death. They're all
we have—in words. But silence, or pure song,
such as the angels sing! Where is the fault
but in words, where there is no fault at all?

               Prayer is to be—wordless—as the flight
of birds, *orare poetica*: one
as water is to warm rain and the sea;
unmoving as the moon one summer night
in June; fluid as light in all the suns.
To pray is not to mean but to be.

Psalms for Skeptics

they that wasted us required of us mirth

A sense of humor helps. There is a man
who saw his family last in Auschwitz—
his mother and his sister waving, father
coughing life away; and he never smiles;
never cracks a joke, never laughs at one:
but he says a sense of humor helps.
His name is Eliezer: "God is my help."
God never said a word; He never cracked
the heavens to come down; was never jealous
of His power of life and death. In fact,
observing from Upstairs, God shook His head:
"It could be worse." I said, How could it be?
Six million of Your chosen people dead?
"It could be worse," He said. "It could be me."

Psalm 137

How shall we sing the Lord's song in a strange land?

How can we sing a song of David here?
The aiders and abettors of abuse
do their worst by denying it—the truth—
the one thing victims need after it's over—
or it's never over. And we should sing
uplifting glory, hallelujah songs
for the begging legless, truth marching on
without them? Let's beat a green tambourine
for the nations' dance of death by carbon,
and of course the germs and chemicals wait
for the Big Lady to sing. Sing God's songs?—
for the skeletons clinging to the gates—
a Kaddish for the sin of Joy—
for David, apple of Jehovah's eye.

Psalm 138

Before the gods will I sing praise unto thee.

What gods are we imagining? "Divine
beings" according to *Tanakh*—not cars
or electronics—idols—but creatures
sharing in the empyrean sublime.
Not angels. Not the morning stars that sang
together when the universe was made.
Are the psalmists, or Calvinists mistaken?—
or the notion of a lonely God wrong?
Is there a society of Jesus—
rank on rank a host of heaven, faces
veiled with adoration in the Presence
of the Holy One—beings we have seen,
hands that move through our world, familiar voices,
bent toward the mad at the hour of our death?

Psalm 138

In the day when I cried thou answerdst me.

Reason speaks against it, experience
is for it: the hand of God to help us,
to heal us, "perfecting that concerneth"
us. But why does experience itself
not accord with reason? Surely it could
be made to, for reason is the mind's fool.
Experience is never understood
without a third hand to use the tool
its way. Reason is the smoothness of words,
experience the rough walk of large birds—
those bold crows congregating in my trees,
swaggering on four-inch stilts at the curb,
hopping on and off the street where one lies
dead, reverent and mysterious as priests.

Psalms for Skeptics

The Lord will perfect that which concerneth me.

He will not leave me unfinished, in doubt,
a sparrow banging the panes of my brain;
He will reach into the little song, the throat
of my bewilderment, and pull me out.
But will I flutter to the Wheel again?
Is God's perfection slow—the tree of time
long-leafing, life progressing in sublime
procession through the hesitating veins?

Or are the myriads God's little schools,
dimension on dimension, room to room
through mansion after mansion of the soul:
one life on earth, then on to what we thought
was heaven—the bird released toward the moon,
but rounding to the air by which it's caught?

Psalm 138

thou wilt revive me

The heart will stop. The lines on the machines
will flatten like dogs, and the nurses
will look the other way. The last shall be first—
the last one I thought would die; and my dreams
will be the realest being of me—"dead
as earth," Lear said—a dream stretching up
into the mind that made it, catching up
to thoughts faster than light that left my head
when I was a boy on a hill; a young
man in college; a worrier in church
pewed to prayer: visions of escape. Well here
it is, you got out. Where are you now, Son?
The place I left you, where the river turns
from light to blue, and the wild geese appear?

Psalm 139

O Lord, thou hast searched me, and known me.

A cat regards me as I write: all black,
her eyes pale green as the eyes of a poet
on another planet. She sits, stays back
a careful ell; she is wild and homeless
as the Son of Man. Her lids droop, dismissive,
bored, but the body's gathered on a dime.
She is looking through all my hidden sins;
she yawns, opening her mouth like a lion,
incisors that slit the tissues of birds.
Her claws could scratch my thoughts across the sky
but her blank calm is too perfect for words.
All we want is to be seen, understood.
Jesus loves me. What she sees is a fool;
they are everywhere here, putting out food.

Psalm 139

You know that I have been nominated
for the Pulitzer Prize. Was Solomon
a king? Did he nibble pomegranate
with an intellectual Sheban queen?
What did his father David think, who loved
excessively, both God and man, and killed
for women—did he think his son was saved
from bloodguilt by his sophistication
and ennui; or did he write poetry
for him, laments and absaloms of grief?—
winning, for his psalms but not for belief,
the Pulitzer. If David had been Greek
it would have meant laurel. He was a Jew.
If he wrote, there was nothing else to do.

Psalms for Skeptics

Thou hast . . . laid thine hand upon me.

The touch of hand, the Rabbi's hand—the sick
sinking in their sheets twenty miles from land
arise and take their cots like chrysalis
to show the world; the stone-staring dead stand
like lilies of the valley. Imagine.
Look at the little girl—a clutch of sticks
and shivering in pulled-to-pieces skin,
clothed in flies her mother listlessly flicks:
touch her; let us lay our hand upon her
though you are no rabbi—neither am I—
and we are in love with a different world:
touch her with our white hand before she dies
and like a moth flutters into sheer dust,
our moon faces the last light in her eyes.

Psalm 139

And touch her twenty year old brother, too,
as he lies in his crib; touch his forehead
round as the Pacific seen from the moon,
large as a basket that holds peasants' bread—
here in the white room, rows along each wall,
the born alone, turned by the touchless trained,
each head a large and nearly faceless ball
dreaming shapes, colors, touch, awake—brains
where our explanations are milky noises
and a hand is The Lord God Almighty.
There's a lot of time. This is no crisis.
God is good; whatever will be will be.
But lay that shrinking hand upon him now,
upon that smooth eternal brow.

Psalms for Skeptics

Lay your hand upon me now. I need you.
I'm a sick man with the soul of a boy;
I am uncertain—don't know what to do—
am afraid of being taken away
to a hospital, then put in the ground.
Those things will happen. There is no escape
into the immortality of psalms—
no getting on a train, riding away
to the West. Hell, I could die out West. Why
can't I accept it? Your hand is enough.
I can feel it.
                Get the poem inside.
It's all I've got.
                The poem is a cup;
hold it in front of you—beg, little boy—
death, a little sip, very weak, of joy.

Psalm 139

"Listen to your body," Jesus says—
the Jesus at my bed. He talks to me
these days when I am sick and brave,
touches my head. What does the body say?
*I'm tired. Don't take me to Texas; I might
die there. Let's just stay home and rest.* Okay,
no trips for awhile, just bumps in the night,
pious oatmeal and an apple a day.
So far, so good, but Jesus doesn't leave.
His hand hovers. Is that hole in the wrist
closed? I feel the breath of his moving sleeve
and close my eyes. It all feels like a gift—
even the rain today on the soft streets
outside, and my hands on the flannel sheets.

Psalms for Skeptics

"Be patient," Jesus says. Which is easier
to say, *Be patient* or *Take up your bed
and write?* But my bed is very heavy.
Lincoln died on it, and the old Confederacy
expired between its lazy cotton sheets.
Civilization gave up its Goethe
the day its posts were driven. It was carved
from olive by a suspicious Odysseus,
Sinatra sipped his last scotch and soda
here, and here the last mad pacifist starved.
They lowered this sinner through the rafters.
Patience should be easier but it's not,
for what is rhythm step by step but clotted
time, and what is rhyme but *What comes after?*

Psalm 139

Jesus knows what he's doing. What is doubt
but experience—just the same as faith—
the experience we have figured out.
The difference is the element of patience.
So Jesus sits down with the score and waits
for the Fates and Muses to get it sorted;
but it's a day that takes a lot of saving.
He'll be ready. When the last track's recorded
by the Angel in that many-splendored
book, you and I will play the realms of gold.
You'll croon and I'll be a bitter-ender
drummer—though all I know is rock and roll.
You're a Stratocaster, I'm a Fender:
The Waiting Patient Potentates of Soul.

Psalms for Skeptics

That'll be the day. Love the midnight shift
but oh boy, love makes a fool of you—
a fool's paradise with your shaky hips
if you're going there looking for Peggy Sue.
Rave on, take your time, think it over Baby
if you're wishing, for love not fade away.
It doesn't matter if it's made of maybe,
but if you're looking for someone to love
don't put your faith in a heaven above.
True love's ways get stronger every day
not somewhere, somewhere, up there in the sky
but down here on the levee in my Chevrolet.
Better get your piece of American pie
because the plane goes down and the music dies.

Psalm 139

If I make my bed in hell, behold, thou art there.

"There is no place that does not see you," Rilke
wrote of art, and even hell has been made.
Thank God! I feared I would be somewhere else
at death, alone as my clothes; for the grave,
it's said, is empty space: "none there embrace."
But death is the Wailing Wall, all that's left
of a child's temple. Small folded notes placed
in its spaces are durable as dust
in the lungs. Grief is the blind eye of God—
hope's bones rolled into a stone wall of Why.
The New City rots with every body,
but even in hell Jerusalem rises,
its blinding torso imagined into truth,
for "there is no place that does not see you."

Psalms for Skeptics

If I take the wings of the morning

Will I rise like Jesus if I take these
wings? If I drink enough of my own poems
will I numb my mouth to the hook, and breathe
water? Can I row to Eden on dreams
of the Empyrean, interpreted
by the spindly, featherless stroke of these
wings? Or in the end will I just be dead
with all the paper floating in the stream?
Answer it yourself, is what the Father
says—whose Spirit spake by the prophets, holy
and invisible—whose Ghost is talking
in flowers, in the cruciform snow rose.
You answer it, the seventy-year itch;
work it out yourself; answer; live with it.

Psalm 139

When I awake, I am still with thee. (Ash Wednesday)

And when I don't awake, will the long night
in non-being be radiant with thee;
and will non-reading of this poetry
become its place of everlasting life?
When this page is burned, who will hold the light
to read it by? How can anything be,
when there's no-one, nowhere, nothing, to see?
What is there in darkness to be made bright?

You walk toward your death. You do not answer.
The white-eyed judge wants to know who you are.
You are ashes on foreheads of the dead,
ashes only a universe could write.
Lord, you are ashes read by candlelight
on every page, on every sacred head.

Psalms for Skeptics

the darkness and the light are both alike to thee

But as for us, the dark and light are two,
these two: the silver and the fisherman—
one a shadow on the water (the man),
the other particle and wave (the who)—
until the sportsman finally falls asleep
and wades the icy Montana river.
He wears no waders but he can't shiver
without a body, though he hears and sees

the wordless whine of a line through water—
one end wrapped on an overeager hand
quick to jerk the quarry in; the other
through the mouth of a cold-blooded steelhead
arcing hard across the flooding spring stream—
light in the vision, dreamer in the dream.

Psalm 140

preserve me from the violent man

The violent bear all of us away—
the schoolyard poor, and sitting presidents,
and Jesus Christ by thousands every day.
Have we become too numerous to mention
except in round numbers—creeping millions
sacrificed by Pilate's tidy cleansing,
comforted by all our true religions?
Is prayer just pretend? Where will it all end—
in a nuclear wrap-up of the globe?
There's disagreement in Jerusalem,
so Pilate's soldiers find a dirty robe,
slap it on the rabbi's shredded back, grin,
and press a crown of thorns onto his head.
"Not again!" his mother cries. "Not again!"

Psalms for Skeptics

When Robert Kennedy was shot and killed
the northern lilacs crowded toward my doorway
shedding petals like old women and saying
that it couldn't happen twice. Hope's a drill
in your hero's head, his throat, through his wrists,
because the violent have abandoned
hope; they're drunk on despair as if they planned
the thirstiness of prayer. They go to kiss
their savior goodbye in Gethsemane
as long as Jesus sweats drops of blood first;
it gets them out of bed on a bad day.
Whatever is bad can always get worse.
Thy will be done and what must be must be:
other prayers, the violent bear away.

Psalm 140

But you pray anyway and why you do
no one can say except perhaps the dead.
They are answers to prayer. They floated through
the eye of the needle, Jerusalem's
gate, and they talk with each other like old
friends about the old days—when they were young
in green pastures, and the Good Lord would hold
them in the hollow of his hand like emeralds,
and Irish blessings were the mother tongue.
So St. Patrick's Day always falls in Lent
like cold stout that hits the glass with a click.
Fill them up—fill the cradles again!
Ah, it's life it is, makes a fellow think;
but it's death, you know, makes a fellow drink.

Psalm 141

Let the righteous smite me

My students sit cross-legged in the sun,
releasing from the wheel of birth and death.
The Twelve are divided, but I am One:
I am Atman, the universal Breath.
I serve my body broken in their hands,
pour out the blood of my companionship:
I am attached to all the myriads
I call forth. I warm the betrayer's lips,
I raise the softened sleepers in the night;
I am the craving plaiter of my crown.
When the red slayer slays Jesus the Christ
I love the hammerer who nails me down,
  and I am bound upon a wheel of fire—
  across the cross of heaven and desire.

Psalm 142

refuge failed me

My eyes, my hearing, everything is gone.
I stoop under the crossbeam of a cross.
The memory of fishing must belong
to someone else's life, to something lost.
I bend on a bridge with my fishing rod,
and smoking Roman soldiers circle in
around the bait looking up. Oh my God,
my God, where did any of this begin?
What did I do wrong? Are minnows no good
here all of a sudden? The rod's slick as hell;
the walkway's alive because the tarred wood
is rolling on the current like a bell.
I can't go back any more or get ahead.
The river swims around me like the dead.

Psalm 143

> *Teach me to do thy will; for thou art my God: thy spirit is good; lead me into the land of uprightness.*

I used to sit by the river sometimes
and not fish, just watching the water going
by, happy it seems but not knowing why.
A rhyme can tie like a knot in a line
before you know it or want it to: cut
it and put it in a new river?
You never cast into the same river
twice. The old God dies—no ifs, ands, or buts—
every time you pray a new prayer, but
surely God's goodness remains—just the way,
the river, changes. I'd like to stay put
awhile again but time speeds up with age
and you can't sit and you can't stay to chat
and the fish stop hitting just like that.

Psalm 143

I remember the days of old

My dad would take me to watch the Milwaukee
Braves play in County Stadium, Sunday
only, his day off. We would always stay
until the last out, to be sure we saw
all that could be seen of the Great Team: Mathews,
Aaron, Warren Spahn, and Lew Burdette—Spahn
especially. Soon they would all be gone
and it seemed that Dad, a pessimist, knew.

I liked Matthews, a stand up guy. Throw right,
bat left; he was one of a kind. I had
his card but didn't want to play third base.
Too hot. Dad, a catcher in the long night
before I knew him, puts on the chest pad,
the mask, pats my head and walks away.

Psalms for Skeptics

I dreamed of Dad the other night: he'd gone
that morning, died. Here is the cup he touched;
and the robe he'd sometimes wear: here it lies.
The poem I never wrote with my eyes
can't be written now. In the Afterlife,
if he's waiting there, he might be whistling
and tossing a ball—though I never saw
him do that. Just thinking of it makes him
seem like someone else. I used a black bat,
light enough to swing fast: my other self,
in playing trim, says Let's play a little
catch, but he was a busy physician
and seldom smiled. I wish I could wish him,
and that if he wanted to he could hit it a mile.

Psalm 143

But I think Dad is waiting with a ball
and he'll toss it to me, his big galoot
with the heavy bat and the pinstripe suit,
and I'll slug it over the right field wall
in that imaginary house I've built
with help from Matthew, Aaron, Luke, and Spahn.
I miss him. I missed him when he was gone
to work, and what I missed I've tried to fill
in, but how that field used to look so green,
perfectly bright green, and the neat infield—
basepaths where no spikes had cut a single
crumb, and home plate white and sharp as a dream.
See, all of it was real, no dream: they'd hit
those balls with cracks like shots. We'll find our seats and sit
on Sunday afternoon and watch the last home team.

Psalm 143

I am thy servant

I am a Chooser of the Slain, a watcher
of the waters for the rising silver
fish, a walker where the young soldiers fought;
and I dream of a Yule-like Valhalla,
tables rowed by familiar Norwegians
and the linen-crisp Host with arms outspread—
I choose him, the quiet fatherly friend
with the golden ball, the first of the dead
to enter this hall. He visited me
when my soul was overwhelmed like a mourning
dove in a willow where the river runs:
I saw him. I am a green olive tree
where the last will and testament is born,
where the light starts that puts out the blindness of suns.

Psalm 143

destroy all them that afflict my soul

Were you there when they nailed me to the tree?
I think you were; I never believed
you hanged yourself. The way you loved me
showed that you survive. I think the nails stung
a little; then you moved on. The money
helped. You adored me, you and your devil:
you can't betray a stranger. Heaven and hell
poured out of your lies like blood and honey.

Were you there when they laid me in the tomb?
Oh, sometimes it causes me to tremble
like an ocean—remembering the Sea
of Galilee, how it shone in the evening
like love in the eyes. You threw that big stone
over this hole like God's discarded throne.

Psalms for Skeptics

You looked me in the eyes and lied to me,
repeating the Apostles' Creed with feeling:
Father, Son (that's me; really it's all me),
and Holy Ghost—which you turned me into
with that kiss in the garden. What is sin
these days, now that I am gone? Who can you
betray for anything like the same ruin?
I flatter myself. There's always Buddha—
and when the last Mohammed hears the bell
you can wrap it up by betraying yourself.
But you won't hang yourself for chumping me;
you'll tell your friends and go to therapy.
You can't help it; your parents are at fault
always; they named you Judas, after all.

Psalm 143

The fiddler's out of work, you used to say;
the one you insult is the one you pay.
You know the Tempter drives a heavy car;
the devil you serve is the one you are.
But I know all this is academic:
betrayal's nothing if not systemic—
you've got temptation running in your loins.
You would refuse but why waste all those coins.
I was your Jesus, Judas, through and through;
but I knew you do what you need to do.
The Disciples didn't know which was which:
who knows the Son from the son of a bitch?
You got what you wanted and so did I:
a god you could kill with a little lie.

Psalms for Skeptics

If Hitler is in heaven so are you,
the Nazi and the suicidal Jew:
Iscariot, J. and Schickelgruber, A.—
two mouthfuls for the gatekeepers to say.
You both were given license to kill:
if one don't get me then the other one will.
The Austrian invented the Big Lie—
or thought he did, but you were first, and I
tasted its fatality—kosher salt
on bitter herbs; and don't say Oy gevalt,
you bastard, because it is no joke
when a child of God goes up in smoke.
I'm angry, just in case you couldn't tell.
Where's the justice? Where's the hottest seat in hell.

Psalm 143

In time to come the forty days of Lent
will slide on piety like myrrh ointment
in lines of Latin from Rome to Venice—
and none to see the fury or the menace
but John, stone blind from staring at the sky,
a lunatic with Judgment in his eyes:
he knows the inning and he knows the score—
my horses pounding pestilence and war;
and when they're done there's always room for a little more.
My gloves are punctured and my spells won't heal;
my trigger finger's on the seventh seal.
I'll swing the rugged lightning like a cross
if Father lets you motherfuckers off.

Psalms for Skeptics

I am thy servant

And then I saw everything that passes—
what is past and is to come: judgment rolled
together like a scroll—a small white soul
with a world of eyes like angel faces;
and in the center, light. Then two were there:
two holding hands, and one was Death: her eyes
knew me; and the other, a breathing Christ.
And then the spell divided into air
and I am here alone. Where would we go
without Death? I bend my head, close my eyes,
but no voice comforts me. Death's smile is kind
as she steps from vision. Her dress is blue
like the Mother of God and I know the face.
"Walk with me," she says. Mother Mary, full of grace.

Psalm 144

> *Blessed be the Lord, my strength, which teacheth my hands to war, and my fingers to fight.* (Holy Saturday)

So Jesus took Ruth's bat along to hell
and belted Satan's balls out of the park.
He waved a fan of tickets in an arc
for Sunday's game: the Field of Asphodel
was finished now and all were welcome there.
Standing at the plate he looked like God,
handsome as horses on Kentucky sod,
beautiful as silver in winter air.

I want your autograph on a clean slate:
You are the Resurrection and the Life.
Tomorrow will be the game of our dreams:
two out, bases loaded, last of the ninth,
a brute on the mound for the other team,
the fans on their feet—the first and the late—
three runs behind and Jesus at the plate.

Psalm 145

Great is the Lord, and greatly to be praised.

The snow in Lent is merciful and kind,
a gentle truth by nature told in simple
majesty, and a drawing-down of blinds
inside the Nazarene's eyes; a richness
of futility like blackbirds walking
on blank snow, etching thin hieroglyphics
for us to read after the Egyptians
have folded their long hands and stopped talking.
Look at it in the trees and on the rising
crocuses, violet and blue in white,
gutsy as hell, believing in nothing but
standing up in the cold, mummified dirt.
Snow is a book of the dead, the last word
covering Easter like the end of thought.

Psalm 145

Thou openest thine hand, and satisfiest the desire
of every living thing.

I miss my angel; I miss the angel
of my dreams—a snow angel with a child
inside. Christ is dead. They pulled the square nails
and bent the chalky figure like a sail
folded in their arms. Where were the angels?
Snow in Los Angeles: the actors stop
and pray; traffic is platelets in dead veins;
Chinese helicopters tilt their last chop
and the country is saved. Our God is faithful
despite what the Romans did to Jesus.
But just once for the child to come again,
to make a difference, to give me one
more chance, to tell me how cold heaven was
before there were days, and saviors, and suns.

Psalms for Skeptics

> *The Lord is nigh unto all that call upon him,*
> *to all that call upon him in truth.*

So this is how it ends?—a slump in snow,
the Holy Corpse stuffed under a snow fort
with boys' rubber boots stubbing the frozen
eyes? They pelt each other in a cold war,
slowing down like toy train engines as time
becomes deliberate, the asteroid
working out co-ordinates on its line
to Earth. The storied element of choice
is small: throw the snowball or not? Seconds
remain. Can't ask for much on a small globe
consisting basically of molten iron.
If the rock misses and the boys are done
early, there is still the corpse in the snow.
The Lord is nigh. The Lord is really nigh.

Psalm 146

While I live will I praise the Lord

The "while I live" is the uncertain part,
but I'm forgetting that for just today,
forgetting fatal haltings of the heart,
forgetting Lent, and forgetting that praise
is an absurdity. I am Birthday
Boy and I am grateful enough for that
to whistle up the first day of spring, pray
some robins into line and tell them what
a privilege it is to be alive.
I can cause this. I can make the tulips
come to attention with crisp Dutch salutes,
and order up a clean sun for the day.
 Anything is possible today; war
 is peace, and death means maybe one year more.

Psalms for Skeptics

The Lord openeth the eyes of the blind

We were not so always. We were not blind
in the canyons of desire that first day,
the Big Bang, when all today's light was made—
neon, phosphorous, LCD, sublime.
We saw it all—Sinatra in the wings
humming, the Mormon Tabernacle Choir
trying on their black-and-whites, Macy's buyers
wiggling their fingers, all the swag and bling
of pro athletics coming into being
from a tiny, tiny start, visible
all at once—no need to guess how bad things
relate to good ones in the big picture—
the crucifixion and the sweet stable
an expanding, illuminated blur.

Psalm 146

It's all about birth: it's the Earth's purpose.
Death is the crazy Catholic in the room
votived with Zen monks. She's universal
and all these enlightened Buddhists are doomed,
but she's bizarrely out of place, devout
when everyone else is matter-of-fact,
and not laughing when all the lights go out.
What are the colors that constitute black?
What is the riddle that answers you back?
Enlightenment slaps you in the face. Death
rises from the center of the lotus,
birth is the end of all things, and the breath
of the Eternal claps its one hand dust
to dust. Wake up! You, Lazarus, come forth!
This is Jesus calling; this is the earth.

Psalm 147

He healeth the broken in heart

Did Jesus, pale and faint, inhale at first,
and like Alcestis did he hesitate
before he ventured through that granite gate,
unwrapping yards of frankincense and myrrh?
Did his side pain him once he was awake,
his swollen face on the Shroud of Turin
unrecognizable even to him?
Did the Son of God rise, or was he raised?

It isn't over, is it? It's Holy
Week until we sing the Hallelujah
Chorus in church. The smell of spring last week
was a lie: snow and cold are back today
lacing the violet flowers in the yard.
There is no beauty like mortality.

Psalm 147

"Don't wish them back," my mother used to say—
the dead; they'll feel the tug and be unhappy
where they are. They and we are in a trap.
Don't feel. We're on our own. Better that way.
What is it breaks the heart but resignation
to the facts, forced disuse?—washing the sheets
and making up the bed—folding up grief
and throwing the plastic cup he used away.

But Mary Magdalene can't get to sleep.
The night is so long and there is nothing
to learn any more. Her body rises;
she goes out; the night is quiet and deep.
Again she weeps her selfish suffering,
and her eyes swim with unrepentant blindness.

Psalm 148

praise him in the heights

The evidence at first was emptiness—
the tomb of Jesus empty as the question
"Why?" Someone took the body; two men ran
and the younger reached the cave first but then
hesitated. The linen wrappings lay
disheveled but the napkin for the head
was rolled precisely as the dead rabbi
would have done it. "They've taken him away,"
beloved Mary said. But the men knew.
And then she saw him and he spoke her name.
Let's go to the tomb. I will outrun you
if I can, but you touch the napkin, you
pick up the wrappings. Whatever you say,
I will write. I will write, but you will do.

Psalm 148

And two by two we'll go, and two by two
we'll meet Him there; and Mary, she can ask
if He is really Jesus who was crucified,
our Teacher, and she can put her right hand,
a finger of her hand, to the bright sleeve—
and I will write it down I promise; I
will put it into words and will believe,
and no one will ever have to ask "Why?"
again. Remember how that man born blind
laughed when Jesus touched his eyes? So do I.
My eyes are swimming with angels in light,
and I hear him say "Mary" as if I
were there; and I hear her say "Rabbuni!"
Let us hold hands, you and she, He and I,
ascending, flying, rising through the sky.

Psalms for Skeptics

Praise Him in the heights. By God's heaven, let
us praise Him. Do you know what this means? Do
you? We haven't lost Him. He was dead—dead
really, and do you know what?—if you knew,
you could calm me down because I don't know.
All I know is that we have Jesus back,
and you can figure it out—you can go
through the Scriptures and figure out exactly
what to call Him. All I can think of now
is to go fishing. You know how the light
leaps off the lake in the morning? That's how
I feel. I could walk on the water right
now, I feel so light. Praise Him in the heights.
Praise Him forever, always. Praise Him now.

Psalm 149

Sing unto the Lord a new song.

A river goes where it flows, but a lake stays.
My name is John; I call myself Beloved
of the Lord, who is risen from the dead
these many years. When I was just a boy
my cousin Jesus took me from the lake
in Galilee and set me in this river
of the stars, and in it I have lived
til I am light and wonderful with age.
Let me sing upon my bed, looking up
at the stars—a new song now. I would go
where I have not written yet, and not sung—
a lyric mad with Jesus and the Holy
Ghost, a lyric beginning with the Word,
and the Word is God, for I have seen the Lord.

Psalms for Skeptics

he will beautify the meek with salvation

I raise the flyrod in my dream, and crack
the river Jordan just before the sky
alights in red. The Beast's fuming saliva
begins to rain across the Horses' backs.
A rising peal of incandescence runs
across the earth, trees wither in the reek
of blowing chemicals, and sudden streaks
of viruses feather across the sun.

This is what I see: the last humanity
razoring themselves across their thin wrists
and the grieving, unoffending meek
sitting in the river. The saints in bliss
and all the violent carried away
walk robed in white by the glittering lake.

Psalm 149

The world's a river and heaven's a lake.
We fish for glory in the stream of vision
but it all pours like the soul into space;
yet in the darkness I hear singing risen
from the granite black of uncreated
dark, and the stone rolls away. Light, pure light!
You hear it; everything is penetrated
by the sound of light. My name is John. I
am every name, one after another,
the meekest, last in the long, limping line,
and the foremost of the Sons of Thunder:
whatever happens to you, it is mine.
The poor, with dust and ages in their eyes,
bow to water, and beautiful arise.

Psalm 150

praise him with the psaltery and harp

The angels sing somewhere beyond our ears
alleluias tender and tremendous
above the firmament, above the years,
where beginnings round on the never-ending—
above the waters where the stars come out
of thought, and Grampa dreams of glistening fish.
Above the boiler room of physics, doubt,
and angleworms, fresh crayons in a dish
are ready to color a new Atlantis
whenever we are ready for another
descent, and notes of the lake of heaven
glimmer like fish in the river of mothers.
 Master, after this short singing's end,
  give us back the harp and we'll start again.

www.ingramcontent.com/pod-product-compliance
Lightning Source LLC
Chambersburg PA
CBHW062002180426
43198CB00036B/2146